BEFORE
THE
VOWS

The Christian Approach to Premarital Sex

JULES KOMI ADATOR

BEFORE THE VOWS
Copyright © 2025 by Jules Komi Adator

ISBN: 978-1-4866-2679-3
eBook ISBN: 978-1-4866-2680-9

Word Alive Press
119 De Baets Street Winnipeg, MB R2J 3R9
www.wordalivepress.ca

WORD ALIVE
—P R E S S—

Cataloguing in Publication information can be obtained from Library and Archives Canada.

CONTENTS

INTRODUCTION

PREMARITAL SEX—IN its forms of intimate kissing and casual, uncommitted sexual intercourse—seems to be taken for granted nowadays by many young people in our society. This is certainly the assumption we see in the media. In fact, these young people presume there is nothing wrong with them enjoying each other sexually, especially when they take contraceptive precautions to avoid unwanted pregnancy and sexually transmitted infections (STIs)

It is also difficult to think of friendship between young men and women that doesn't end in sexual intercourse. Some young people may well be self-disciplined in this matter. However, under the influence of their peers, alcohol, and economic difficulty, they may find themselves in sexual encounters.

What factors account for such sexual behaviour among youth today, including Christian youth? We must pose the unavoidable question: is it morally right for young people to engage themselves in premarital sex? That is the principal question I will discuss in this book.

Earlier in my life, my missionary training took me to the Archdiocese of Lagos in Nigeria where I went through a year of pastoral experience at the St. Joseph Parish, situated in Gowon Estate. There I had the opportunity to work with youth groups of the parish, namely the Catholic Youth Organization, Altar Servers, Block Rosary Crusade, Boy's Brigade, Vocation Guild, St. Mary's Choir, and Junior Presidia of the Legion of Mary. It was an exciting time for me.

Though a seminarian, I was a young person myself at the time. They saw me as being one of them. We grew close and were able to share openly about their personal problems and interpersonal issues.

Apart from what these young men and women shared with me, my own observations confirmed the truths found in this book. As they interacted on a daily basis, whether during choir practice, prayer meetings, sports, or liturgical rehearsals, I saw them build friendships between each other, men and women together. Unfortunately, these friendships often proved to be sexual and erotic. On a specific occasion, I also observed that such a relationship resulted in fights between two young men.

From this, I concluded that the topic of premarital sex deserves special attention and investigation.

I took my time to interview many of these young people. One of them, a twenty-year-old active member of the Catholic Youth Organization, told me,

> Brother, I believe you can understand me better than the senior priests. Maybe you do not know that I have a girlfriend in St. Mary's Choir. We have been together now for two years. We started well and have been getting on well, but lately I became suspicious of her. Unfortunately, it has come to my notice that she has been going out with another man in the same choir. Upon hearing this, I was so annoyed to the point of fighting with him. I find it necessary to fight so he may leave the girl alone for me, because I was the first to befriend her and she is mine.

Another youth confessed to me that she had three boyfriends and loved them all. She shamelessly declared that she was able to manage them without their knowledge; each had a day when they met and hung out.

Still another told me that he had to have more than one girlfriend in order to prove his manhood.

Considering all that I heard and observed from these youth, I was able to pinpoint an ever-growing pastoral problem. They engaged in premarital sex in all its forms from petting and kissing up to sexual intercourse. They themselves acknowledged this.

An eighteen-year-old member of the Legion of Mary in Lagos explained, "If you do not do it [have sexual intercourse], your friends will say you are not a full human being."

The sad reality is that they take it for granted that there is nothing wrong with making love to one another while they are still teenagers. I find this situation deplorable. But nothing would ever change if I kept on lamenting and didn't take concrete action. Only strong pastoral measures can pave the way for an acceptable and dignified sex life among our Christian youth.

When a malaise is identified in a person, a cure is needed. If not a cure, then at least a preventative measure.

In this book, I have no pretension of offering something new. But I would like to say old things in a new way, and perhaps a fresh perspective. In order to convey my message, I have drawn insight from written sources, my own pastoral experience, and interviews I conducted with youth. I hope to contribute, in a modest way, to the promotion of a culture of sexual self-discipline among youth in general and Christian youth in particular.

CHAPTER ONE

HUMAN SEXUALITY

AND

BEHAVIOUR AMONG YOUTH

Let no one have contempt for
your youth, but set an example for those who believe, in
speech, conduct, love, faith,
and purity. (1 Timothy 4:12)

EVERY HUMAN IS a sexual being. Thus, it follows that many of our human relationships and behaviours are sexually oriented.

But to what extent can these be tolerated, or even accepted, by our own human codes of morality, not to mention the code of God's precepts? The ideal expression of our sexuality does not cause any harm to us. However, when it is used prematurely and excessively, as we shall see is being done among youth today through casual and random sex, it becomes not only immoral but also detrimental to one's physical, emotional, and spiritual health.

THE REALITY OF HUMAN SEXUALITY

Sexuality is part and parcel of the human personality. It is also a divine relational gift shared between us. It needs to be approached with a sense of deep appreciation, respect, and wonder.

In this regard, one can recall the definition provided by Gerald Coleman: "Sexuality refers to a fundamental component of human personality in and through which we as male and female experience our relatedness to self, others, the world and even God."[1]

Sexuality is like a power that prompts us from within, calling us to personal as well as spiritual growth and drawing us out from ourselves to form interpersonal relationships and make serious commitments to others. It causes us to embrace all the qualities peculiar to a genuine human relationship—namely sensitivity, mutual understanding, intimacy, openness to one another, compassion, sympathy, and mutual support.

The Congregation for Catholic Education rightly perceives this relational dimension of human sexuality:

> Sexuality is a fundamental component of personality, one of its modes of being, of manifestation, of communicating with others, of feeling, of expressing and of loving human love. Therefore, it is an integral part of the development of the personality and its educative process.[2]

---

[1] Gerald Coleman, *Human Sexuality: An All-Embracing Gift* (New York, NY: Alba House, 1992), 10.

[2] Sacred Congregation for Catholic Education, *Educational Guidance in Human Love* (Rome, IT: Catholic Truth Society, 1983), 4.

Everyone has the natural ability to love and be loved. Through our sexuality, we are pushed from within towards a particular person of the opposite sex. Love is the driving force behind this movement.

It is important to note that we are not talking merely of bodily functions for performing specific sexual acts. Rather, we're discussing the relational power that leads to the establishment of interpersonal communion between us.

Hence, at the stem of sexuality, love must blossom in order to render it "a dimension of one's restless heart, which continually yearns for interpersonal communion, glimpsed and experienced to varying degrees in this life, ultimately finding full oneness only in God."[3]

The gift of sexuality, in the fullest and richest sense, is to be found when our hearts are open to one another regardless of our race or status. We are not being driven to perform irresponsible acts; sexuality is a force designed by God for the good of all humans, for their maturation towards the completion of God's lovely project for humankind.

One cannot separate a person from their sexuality. It constitutes an integral part of the person because it involves the entire being, enabling them to be relational. In this regard, the exercise of human sexual faculties is ordered towards interpersonal communication rather than the mere satisfaction of drives and compulsions as among animals. On a profound level, human sexuality possesses a spiritual dimension whereby the self reaches towards a deep relationship with God.

---

[3] Coleman, *Human Sexuality*, 10.

This exercise conveys also the possibility of transmitting life, thus ruling out any kind of selfish interest or self-satisfying pleasure. True sexual acts should transcend self-centeredness so we see in others the potential for true communion. Human sexuality is so closely related to the experience of our interpersonal relationships that it eventually permeates every single communication of love.

This is beautifully underlined by Dave Daddy:

> Attached to a person's sexuality is the capacity to feel affection, to delight in someone else, to get emotionally close to another person, to be passionately committed to him or her, to be in love, to be struck by the beauty of another and drawn out of yourself, to become attached to another human being so powerfully that you easily begin measuring your life in terms of what is good for someone else as well as for yourself.[4]

Sexuality should always find its expression in sacrificial love. But when it takes another form, such as when we use others as objects instead of respecting them, we are led down the road of egoism, which impoverishes, frustrates, and at times brutalizes us.

---

[4] Dave Daddy, "What Is Human Sexuality and What Is Normal?" *Catholic Education*. Date of access: October 15, 2004 (http://catholiceducation.org/articles/sexuality/se0002.html).

PREMARITAL SEXUAL ACTIVITY AMONG YOUTH

In 1986, a revolution of students in the northern hemisphere reject-
ed traditional values of sexual behaviour, believing them to be
outdated. They felt those values were incompatible with their new
ways of thinking. This revolution brought sexuality out of its hidden
ghetto into the open arena.

Before this, the traditional conception of sexuality had been
somewhat negative. Sex was considered taboo, not to be dis-
cussed and practiced. This sexual revolution resulted in a change
of mentality about sex. Many people, especially youth, gained the
freedom and courage to indulge themselves without having any
accompanying remorse or guilt.

> The sex revolution however went to the opposite.
> Because of contraceptive, sexual activity could
> now be enjoyed without incurring the responsi-
> bility of parenthood. And sex was now "out in
> the open." Sex could be enjoyed without guilt,
> as well as without responsibility. Sexual freedom
> was reckoned to be part of human freedom,
> which should not be restricted.[5]

The general observation nowadays is that many young people,
even though they're not yet physically, psychologically, or emo-
tionally mature, involve themselves in sexual practices as a way
of enjoying themselves and seeking pleasure. Occasions such as

---

[5] Aylward Shorter, *Celibacy and African Culture* (Nairobi, KE: Paulines Publications
Africa, 1998), 29.

weekend camps and end-of-academic-year parties provide good opportunities for these young men and women to meet and engage in sex.

Some of these sexual experiences can be casual—that, they have intercourse for the sake of curiosity. They may also have random sex, which is sometimes the result of being overtaken by the effects of alcohol. Another form of premarital sex is regular intercourse with different partners, which many young people embrace with joy and without questioning the practice.

These acts of sexual deviance are truly alarming, as Janet Smith observes by naming the factors that account for them:

> Premarital sexual activity is common in many parts of the world and is reported to be on the rise in all regions. In many countries, young women and men are under strong social and peer-group pressure to engage in premarital sex. Moreover, some features of modern life may increase both the desire and opportunity for sexual activity: the mass media, the breakdown of traditional families and mores and increased migration, urbanization and materialism.[6]

The traditional teaching of human sexuality states that any normal sex act should allow for the possibility of procreation. That is the natural consequence of intercourse. But not all forms of

---

[6] Janet Smith, "Premarital Sex," *Catholic Education*. Date of access: October 20, 2004 (http://catholiceducation.org/articles/sexuality/se0002.html).

premarital sex take procreation into consideration, since these acts are enjoyed merely for pleasure. In this way, many young people now believe that sex is the most widely available source of happiness one can attain. They also believe that sex is proof of mutual love.

In reality, premarital sex runs counter to sexual integrity and the unitive dimension of sexuality seen as a source of procreative and nurturing life.

Hence, in order to avoid violating the integrity of the expression of human sexuality, which is only permissible within matrimonial engagement, it is imperative that young men and women who choose to engage in sex question themselves on the following basis:

> Before engaging in premarital expression of genital intercourse, then every person should raise certain questions about his or her prospective sexual partner: e.g.; "can I honestly say that if I ever have a child, it will be with you?" or, "Are you the one I want to be the mother or father of my child?" Or "Are you the one I want to be with, to care for, and to be cared for, for the rest of my life?" In human persons, sexuality cannot be reduced to mere biological or physical realities. All sexual activity, in other words, has a moral consent. Persons who are contemplating premarital intercourse should always truthfully remember that circumstances change, engagements are broken, and promises

are not vows. Words of love do need the strength-
ening that comes from the willing support of the
community of faith and the sacramental grace of
marriage.[7]

SOME CAUSES OF PREMARITAL SEX AMONG YOUTH

It is certain that a good number of young people today are sexually
active before marriage. Why has this trend become so common?
There must be factors that account for such behaviour. Sociologi-
cal, economic, cultural, and physiologic factors have all normalized
these sexual practices that are on the rise today.

Leo Kock, writing in 1960, based his argument on the larges-
cale availability of contraceptives:

> With modern contraceptives and medical advice
> readily available at the nearest drug store or at
> least a family physician, there is no valid reason
> why sexual intercourse should not be condoned
> among those sufficiently mature to engage in it
> without social consequences.[8]

Such an affirmation is a reflection of the real thoughts that
flood the minds of many people today, especially youth. According
to them, the availability of contraceptives provides them with the
opportunity to safely engage in sexual activities.

---

[7] Coleman, *Human Sexuality*, 278.

[8] Leo Kock, "Advice on Sex," *The Daily Illini*. March 18, 1960, 4.

The practice of contraceptive sex has therefore allowed many to separate the act of having sex from the act of having children and bonding with another. It is obvious that young people who have frequent sexual intercourse need not discuss what happens in the event of pregnancy. They do not expect a pregnancy to happen, but if one should occur they are aware that abortion is a commonly practiced option. With this casual attitude, many youth are led to embrace sexual activity at a premature age.

Another factor that needs to be mentioned is the growing prevalence of the free-sex culture. As Gerald Coleman puts it, many of them "live in an anonymous social setting and have *de facto* adopted an attitude that says, my sexual conduct is none of your business."[9] Sometimes even their parents have no control over them and dare not discuss their sexual behaviour. They are vulnerable to peer pressure, which pushes them into experiencing sex. They go so far as to convince one another to taste just like one would test-drive a car before buying one.

The fact that young people are so prone to engage in premarital sex may be due to the publicity surrounding sex in the media, which is made easily available.

> It is uncontroversial to note that our entertainment and media bombard our young people with the message that everyone should be sexually active; that sexual activity is essential to happiness. It also bombards them with sexual stimuli; an enormous number of products are marketed

[9] Coleman, *Human Sexuality*, 271.

> with ads featuring scantily clad seductive women
> or with men and women in romantic, not to say,
> explicitly sexual poses.[10]

Another motive that contributes to premarital sex among youth is the rural exodus, the very common phenomenon that pushes young people from villages to urban settings in the hope of finding greener pastures. Unfortunately, "while the youth exodus towards urban centers increases, the job opportunities there get less. This process creates a vicious cycle of unemployment. Then idleness induces some of these young people to indulge in sexual immorality."[11]

Sometimes young people think they are strong enough to deal with great emotional dependency while avoiding physical intimacy, even when they have indulged in strong drinks. However, even the most committed Christian young people, while under the influence of alcohol, cannot control themselves; consequently, instinct compels them to participate in random sex.

In many other cases, youth who have lost their parents for one reason or another find themselves in a situation where nobody takes care of them. In such circumstances, many young people, especially women, find an easy way out through the immorality of commercial sex, commonly called prostitution.

There is also a physiological factor in the long list of incentives for premarital sex among youth today. In many parts of the world,

---

[10] Janet Smith, "Premarital Sex," *Catholic Education*. Date of access: October 20, 2004 (http://catholiceducation.org/articles/sexuality/se0002.html).

[11] J. Lebubu, "The Youth on the Threshold of the Year 2000," *African Ecclesial Review*. February 1989, 214.

the onset of puberty is coming earlier while the age of marriage rises due to young people spending more time in postsecondary studies. Youth today face a long wait until they are sexually mature. Thus, they often become sexually active before marriage. This phenomenon has been noticed by Gerald Coleman:

> The premarital period (time between puberty and marriage) is a rather recent phenomenon in history and creates an atmosphere that produces an acceptable and conducive environment for sexual expression, especially when people are getting married at a latter age.[12]

The issue of premarital sex among youth can result from transitioning from a more traditional culture to one that is more greatly influenced by modernity, globalization, and urbanization.

CONSEQUENCES OF PREMARITAL SEX AMONG YOUTHS

Premarital sex can be self-destructive when young people indulge in it ignorantly. Among the many risks associated with this immoral behaviour is unwanted pregnancy. In reality, pregnancy in itself is not bad, but it becomes a problem for young women who are neither physiologically nor psychologically prepared for it.

The fact is that many young girls find themselves unexpectedly pregnant after sexual intercourse and then have to carry their pregnancy against their wishes. Because of the shame of carrying an unwanted pregnancy, their lives becomes traumatic for them-

---

[12] Coleman, *Human Sexuality*, 272.

selves, their child, and their families. It leads to many complications for them as young mothers. Sometimes, foreseeing these eventual complications, many such young women drop out of school or opt to terminate the pregnancy by means of an abortion, which is known to be a cause of death and infertility among teen mothers today.

Another negative consequence of premarital sex concerns the realm of emotions. Since the majority of teens know that sexual intercourse is wrong and impermissible at their age, they eventually feel remorse and guilt, which sometimes leads to deep frustration and self-hatred. And the more they indulge in premarital sex, the more guilt they feel. Consequently, the fear and loss of self-esteem and self-respect which result from it can endanger their psychological and mental health.

Considering the fact that most premarital sex among young people occurs in places that aren't secure or private, it has a negative influence on their sexual behaviour later in life. J. Kiura and R. Gitau are then right to say, "Unfavorable conditions plus the fear of discovery can initiate a chain reaction of poor habits and attitudes towards sex which can linger on into marriage with frustrating effects on marital sexual relationships."[13] To these authors, premarital sex is detrimental to the physical and emotional health of young girls because they are forced to carry pregnancies against their wishes. They also run the risk of cervical cancer.

Fidelity is the golden rule in married life, but premarital sex can make this difficult and can lead to extramarital sex. If there is no

[13] Jane M. Kiura, Regina Gitau, and Andrew Kiura, *On Life and Love: Guidelines for Parents and Educators* (Nairobi, KE: Paulines Publications Africa, 1999), 95.

lifelong commitment, a marriage becomes unhappy and may end in divorce. What accounts for this? Past sexual experiences often cause one partner to feel dissatisfied with one's spouse. Such situations preclude the possibility of matrimonial harmony, making divorce inevitable.

Another serious consequence of premarital sex is the increasing risk of cervical cancer among young women. This is made clear in this report from the American Journal of Obstetrics and Gynecology:

> In early adolescence the uterus, the fallopian tubes, the ovaries and the cervix are still developing. The cervix is extremely vulnerable during this time. If exposed to semen it can set the stage for carcinoma of cervix later on in life. Semen contains antigens' that sensitize that cervix and may cause abnormal development when a girl is exposed to it too early, too often and by multiple sexual partners. Research shows that the younger a girl becomes sexually active the more partners she has, and the more frequent the exposure during those years, the higher her chances of contracting cervical cancer between the ages of 40–50.[14]

Premarital sex exposes both young women and men to sexually transmitted infections such as gonorrhoea, syphilis, herpes,

---

[14] Ibid., 97.

chlamydia, and HIV/AIDS, which can result in sterility and even death.

At the spiritual level, premarital sex condemns teenagers to feel guilt for disrespecting their bodies and offending God. Thus they may find themselves alienated from God and feel a kind of boredom with life.

According to author James A. Mohler, "The evidence is that the habit of premarital intercourse can serve to enslave rather than liberate, can gradually reduce enjoyment rather than augment it, and produce neurotic rather than zestful men and women"[15] who are called to experience and enjoy the freedom of the children of God.

Premarital sex, therefore, is a violation of the divine gift of human sexuality because it occurs outside the marital consent of two partners. It is both a violation and transgression of the divine law that restricts sexual intercourse to married couples.

To suggest a solution to the problem of premarital sex among teenagers, one should take into consideration the indispensable contributions of Christian morality and cultural tradition for promoting a realistic and holistic approach to sexuality.

In the next chapter, let us examine what the African traditional heritage holds for us in this regard.

---

[15] James A. Mohler, *Love, Marriage, and the Family: Yesterday and Today* (New York, NY: Alba House, 1992), 131.

CHAPTER TWO

THE UNDERSTANDING
— OF HUMAN SEXUALITY —
IN THE AFRICAN TRADITION

Hear, my son, your father's
instruction, and reject not
your mother's teaching; a
graceful diadem will they be
for your head; a pendant for
your neck. (Proverbs 1:8–9)

MODERN SOCIETIES INCREASINGLY view sexual activity solely in terms of biological gratification and pleasure without serious responsibility. This is contrary to the view of societies in Africa where sexual activity is not only biological but also a matter of religious and social concern. Sex is seen as sacred, signifying one's inner spiritual values.

Sexuality from an African perspective has a threefold dimension: communitarian, religious, and symbolic. In order to take a broader view, we will draw examples from different traditional cultures in Africa.

CONTEXT OF THE COMMUNITY

Communication is an important value in traditional Africa. The sorrow or joy of any community member is shared by every other member. Similarly, one's personal or individual view of sexuality isn't necessarily a private affair, but rather a matter of community concern.

As Bénézet Bujo writes,

> African communities are interested in the sexual lives of all their members, since sexuality is not a private matter. The goal of sexuality is to keep together the community entrusted to us by our ancestors and to bestow ever new life on this community. It follows that the community must prepare young people for a responsible sexual life, psychologically and physically.[16]

This community concern aims to inculcate moral norms in young people, preparing them to engage in decent sexual behaviour that is acceptable in their society. The rites of initiation, for instance, provide the opportunity to teach young men and women the correct and right use of their sexuality. These initiation rites involve the community because a young person's sexual education is oriented towards the whole community's future and continuity.

That is why Bujo insists on the importance of the community in assuring the continuity of life:

---

[16] Bénézet Bujo, *Foundations of an African Ethic: Beyond the Universal Claim of Western Morality* (Nairobi, KE: Paulines Publications Africa, 2003), 59.

> In this community, one of the paramount aspi-
> rations is procreation. Thus, a man who dies
> without progeny falls, in a way, into oblivion. In
> some traditions a piece of charcoal is put into his
> mouth to indicate that the fire of life had died out.
> Procreation is thus a question not only of indi-
> vidual survival, but also of community survival.[17]

The community's interest in the sexual lives of its members is oriented towards the regulation of sexual activity, especially among youth. In reality, sexual activity is not permitted before traditional marriage. It can only happen when community leaders lead young men and women through their rites of initiation.

Some of these initiation rites include proof of sexual maturity. Other rites can be extended even to masturbation, which in the African context isn't meant to be an individual act but a meaningful act performed in the presence of at least two witnesses.

In this regard, the attitude towards sexuality in traditional Africa is procreation-oriented. This rules out all forms of infertility, as underlined by Bujo:

> Infertility and sterility block the channel through
> which the steam of life flows; they plunge the per-
> son concerned into misery, they sever him from
> personal immorality and threaten the perpetuation

---

[17] Bénézet Bujo, *African Christian Morality at the Age of Inculturation* (Nairobi, KE: Paulines Publications Africa, 1990), 108.

> of the lineage. And because the generation of life was a matter of concern to the whole community, there were strong sanctions against people who indulged in sex for selfish reasons. Sexuality and its powers were understood as permeating every level of human existence: interpersonal relationships and matters of ritual. Sexuality was looked upon as mysterious and sacred.[18]

Viewing sexual activity from a communitarian perspective aims to strengthen the bond between families and clans through interpersonal relationships, increasing communication between people and fostering happiness in the community.

Community cohesion is of great importance to Africans and sexuality plays a part in building up the community through hospitality. Bujo explores this idea further:

> Sexuality in the African tradition has succumbed neither to unbridled license nor to the consumer mentality: it aims at building up the community. One must not lose sight of this background, when one encounter a practice that are foreign to western Christianity, for example, the idea that sexuality is a form of hospitality. The tradition in some cultures in Black Africa is that when a friend comes to visit, the husband gives the

---

[18] Benezeri Kisembo, Laurenti Magesa, and Aylward Shorter, *African Christian Marriage* (Nairobi, KE: Paulines Publications Africa, 1998), 127.

> guest his wife for the night, as a sign of friend-
> ship. Among the Masai, the period of initiation
> plays an important role in the sexual community:
> companions in initiation are allowed to have sex-
> ual intercourse with the wives of other members
> of this group. Here too the basic idea is the cohe-
> sion and renewal of the community.[19]

This form of hospitality isn't advisable nowadays due to the prevalence of sexually transmitted infections, including HIV/AIDS, which can be fatal and threaten a community's continuity.

No discussion of the community's interest in sexuality could be complete without mentioning one of the main advantages of this approach. In traditional Africa, all women are given the opportunity to marry in order to enjoy a legitimate sex life. Whether they find themselves in a monogamous or polygamous marriage, which is culturally accepted, the ultimate goal is to prevent women from engaging in any form of prostitution or sexual promiscuity.

THE RELIGIOUS DIMENSION OF SEXUALITY

Traditional Africans are essentially religious people. They carry their religion with them in all their activities—including farming, fishing, and dancing—and artistic works. It is believed that these all carry a religious connotation. Thus, in the words of Aylward Shorter, "pro-creation is essentially a religious obligation, because transmitting life means sharing in the divine prerogative of creation itself."[20] If

---

[19] Bujo, *Foundations of an African Ethic*, 59–60.

[20] Shorter, *Celibacy and African Culture*, 17.

procreation is said to have a religious dimension, it follows that the expression of sexuality is not left out of the religious realm.

According to Peter Kasenene, sexuality has a very significant place in African traditional religion:

> In African religious, sex occupies an important place in social and religious lives of the people and it is associated with many beliefs, practices and taboos. Sex is respected as a channel for procreation, a means to regain the immortality which was lost in the remote past. So, sex is of tremendous religious significance with taboos attached to it. It is believed among Nyakyusa of Tanzania, for example, that sexual fluid is so sacred that it is harmful to babies; and a woman keeps a way from her husband during the nursing period and when she gets involved in a sexual act, she must wash herself thoroughly before getting in touch with the baby. Among the Banyankore, it is believed that adultery committed when a person is in the process of building a house causes death for the partner when they enter the new house. A cleansing ritual is necessary before they occupy the house to avert the danger. Among the Bakiga of Uganda, a parent to intentionally show his or her genital organ to

the child with intention of cursing him or her is
the most efficacious method.[21]

The Ewe people of Togo and Ghana maintain a strong belief in cursing by exposing one's genital organs. For these people, intentionally showing one's private parts to a son, daughter, niece, or nephew while under the influence of anger results in their culture's most powerful curse.

The religious aspect of sexuality is also noted in the fact that sexual activity is sometimes dramatized through dance and art. This ritual sex, according to Aylward Shorter, "symbolizes the fertility of plants and animals as well as humans, and it is a feature of the principle of 'cosmobiology' or the continuity of life and fertility between the different orders of being."[22] The religious dimension of sexuality is also the subject of "dialogue with the future, a communication with the unborn. It made it possible for the unborn to be released into this world."[23]

Even though African tradition holds sexuality dear for its procreative role, it doesn't stop there. Sexual intercourse sometimes stands as the expression of joy for spouses in celebrating significant events that affect their families. Bujo acknowledges the existence of this practice:

---

[21] Peter Kasenene, *Religious Ethics in Africa* (Kampala, UG: Fountain Publishers, 1998), 57.

[22] Shorter, *Celibacy and African Culture*, 21.

[23] Ibid.

A further indication that sexuality aims at more than just procreation is the fact that in many regions particular events are to be sealed or celebrated by sexual intercourse between the spouses, for example, the marriage celebrations of one's children, the appearance of a child's first teeth and also funeral rites.[24]

It is also understood by the Luo people of Kenya that sexual intercourse is a rite of fertility on some occasions.[25]

Human sexuality, from the African perspective, is not just religious. It is essentially sacred.

THE SACREDNESS OF SEXUAL ACTIVITY

The sacredness of sexual activity in traditional Africa does not contradict the community dimension of sexual life. In fact, sexuality in traditional Africa is surrounded by many taboos.

In many African cultures, sexual matters haven't been subjects of discussion between parents and their children, and no less among brothers and sisters of the same family. Anything related to sexuality is sacred and thus held in secret. Intercourse itself is essentially sacred because it has the mysterious characteristic of transmitting life, which finds its origin in God.

In most African societies, such as the Ewe community, it is a great offence to expose one's private parts for pleasure; these organs are honoured for being the gate of new life. Genital organs

---

[24] Bujo, *Foundations of an African Ethic*, 59.

[25] Henry Okullu, *Church and Marriage in East Africa* (Nairobi, KE: Uzima Press, 1990), 16.

or buttocks are therefore mostly covered. Failing to do so constitutes nakedness, which isn't tolerated. To demonstrate the sacredness of sexual organs, people of the opposite sex aren't allowed to mingle freely or have extended physical contact except in the case of sexual intercourse in legal marriage.

According to many customs, only married couples have the right to sexual activity. This is why in traditional Africa many sexual offences—premarital sex, fornication, adultery, rape, incest, and intercourse with animals—are severely punished. It can result in excommunication from one's village. Another consequence is contracting a physical illness or mental derangement.

NORMS OF SEXUAL ACTIVITY

In terms of judging what is appropriate or inappropriate sexual behaviour, the norms vary considerably from one community to the other. However, there are two categories of community: conventionalists and liberals.

For the conventionalist, sexual intercourse is only morally appropriate within the bonds of marriage. Thus, all forms of premarital or extramarital sex—be it oral, heterosexual or homosexual intercourse, or masturbation—are regarded as immoral.

On the other hand, the liberal maintains that sexual intercourse is just one type of human expression and therefore should not be despised. They don't view sex outside of marriage as being immoral, per se, as long as it doesn't violate "pre-existent universally agreed general moral rules and principles."[26]

---

[26] Kasenene, *Religious Ethics in Africa*, 58.

In Africa, the ethical norms pertaining to sexual activity can generally be categorized as conventionalist, maintaining that sexual intercourse is only permissible within traditional and legal marriage. All forms of premarital sex are discouraged, prohibited, and also severely punished.

As Peter Kasenene writes,

> As general principle, in African religious [cultures], sex before marriage is discouraged and severely punished. A girl for example, is expected to be chaste until marriage. For that reason, virginity is highly valued and rewarded. In most African societies, girls are taught to protect their virginity until marriage and never to allow a man to violate it.[27]

Generally speaking, young men need not remain chaste before marriage. However, it is a must for young women, which indirectly forces young men to also keep themselves chaste.

It is very important for young women to remain virginal. A girl who takes the risk of losing her virginity consequently loses respect and dignity and becomes a source of embarrassment to her parents as well as to her peers.

In some cultures, like the Ewe culture, of which I am a product, virginity is so valuable that even betrothed couples who happen to share the same bed, which is common before an official traditional marriage, are not allowed to indulge in intercourse.

---

[27] Ibid., 59.

It is also worth noting that in many African cultures, including my own, intercourse is never to occur outdoors in an open place, such as a beach, field, or wooded area. If this occurs, our people believe that the contact of sperm and vaginal fluid with the earth can make even rich farming land become unproductive. Indeed, it can also prevent rains from falling, producing drought and famine. It is an additional taboo for our people to have intercourse during a woman's menstruation period. The flow of blood during this period is considered to be a sign of impurity, and coming into contact with it is a terrible source of curse and misfortune. However, this is a cultural belief that has not been scientifically proven.

The paramount role intercourse plays in procreation causes some peoples, such as the Yoruba in Nigeria, to use every available means to ensure that engaged persons are truly fertile. It is commonly accepted that a prospective bride must be impregnated before the day of the traditional wedding ceremony.[28]

Under normal circumstances, neither premarital nor extramarital sexual activity has any place in African tradition. However, social conditions sometimes force certain communities, like the Yoruba, to accept the possibility of a man impregnating his fiancée before the actual wedding.[29]

Overall, premarital sex for pleasure is not accepted. The proof of this prohibition is the punishment such acts elicit in some cultures.

---

[28] A. Oyekanmi, "Understanding Sexuality in Yoruba Culture," *Africa Regional Sexuality Resource Centre*. Date of access: September 29, 2004 (http://www.arsrc.org/en/resources/reports/alaba comments.pdf).

[29] Ibid.

> Among the Bakobi of Uganda, the seducer [i.e.
> the young man who has a premarital sexual inter-
> course with a girl] has to pay a heavy fine to the
> girl's families and the king, and the girl is driven
> from home, retained forever as an outcast.[30]

In other cases, such as among the Ewe, a young man who is caught or reported to be the cause of a woman's loss of virginity is automatically compelled to marry her. Among the Swahili of East Africa, the Ewe of Togo, and the Egyptians in general, a bride who is found not to be virginal at the time of first sexual intercourse with her husband, on the very night of their wedding ceremony, is automatically repudiated.[31] But when a groom finds his wife to be a virgin, according to the Akan people of Ghana, he sends a gift to his father-in-law the following morning: a bottle of liquor tied with a white cloth.[32]

Today the ideal of virginity at marriage is hardly taken seriously, apparently because of the belief that everyone has sexual needs that must be fulfilled.[33]

However, African tradition still holds virginity dear. It provides moral norms concerning the who, when, and where of sexual inter-course, as well as punitive directives in order to maintain such

---

[30] I.D. Osabutey-Aguedze, *The African Religion and Philosophy* (Nairobi, KE: Maillu Publishing House, 1990), 160.

[31] Ibid., 161.

[32] Robert B. Fisher, *West African Religious Traditions: Focus on the Akan of Ghana* (Maryknoll, NY: Orbis Books, 1998), 80.

[33] Marjorie Oludhe Macgoye, *Moral Issues in Kenya: A Personal View* (Nairobi, KE: Uzima Publishing House, 1996), 25.

norms. This is the way African tradition regulates and tries to preserve the virginity of young people, especially women: to respect the goal of sexuality and its expression as willed by God, the creator of all things.

CHAPTER THREE

HUMAN SEXUALITY
⸻ ACCORDING TO ⸻
THEOLOGICAL SOURCES

Rejoice, O youth, while you
are young and let your heart
be glad in the days of your
youth. Follow the ways of
your heart, the vision of your
eyes; yet understand regarding all this that God will bring
you to judgment. Banish
misery from your heart and
remove pain from your body,
for youth and black hair
are fleeting. (Ecclesiastes
11:9–10)

FOR ANY THEOLOGICAL reflection on a topic like human sexuality
to be complete, it must be submitted to the scrutiny of the three
sources of theology: the teachings of Holy Scripture, the tradition

of the church, and the magisterium. These sources emerge from different periods of time, but it's worth noting that the last two are dependent on the first. Thus, they are all interconnected.

THE BIBLICAL VIEW OF HUMAN SEXUALITY

The Old Testament view. The Old Testament deals with human sexuality by approaching it in the general context of morality. To those who lived during the Old Testament period, there was no separation between human sexuality and their religious belief.

> The Hebrews saw sexuality primarily in moral terms and they understood morality in the light of their faith in God. Morality thus understood was primarily a way of response to the love of God revealed to them in various covenants God offered them. Thus, the context of morality was religious, and moral requirements were aspects of worship.[34]

The Old Testament views human sexuality as good in and of itself. In fact, the message of Scripture concerning the goodness of human sexuality is to be found in Genesis 1:31, where after creating all things God declared them to be *"very good."* By creating human beings in his image— *"male and female he created them"* (Genesis 1:27), God placed sexuality at the centre of human reality.

---

[34] Ronald Lawler, Joseph Boyle, and William E. May, *Catholic Sexual Ethics: A Summary, Explanation, and Defense* (Huntington, IN: Our Sunday Visitor, 1998), 17.

The fact that God created humans both male and female proves that their sexuality is to be complementary and ordered. After creating them in two genders, God instructed them, *"Be fertile and multiply; fill the earth and subdue it"* (Genesis 1:28). His divine order empowered humans to transmit the very life they had received from God, thus taking part in his own work of creation. It thus becomes evident that human sexuality carries a procreative purpose, with men and women operating as co-creators with God.

The Old Testament provides us with another important insight into the meaning of human sexuality. The Song of Songs portrays human sexuality as good and maintains that sexual union is an occasion of joy and celebration (Song of Songs 6:10–12, 7:1, 8:1). Sexuality therefore also has an erotic function.

However, one shouldn't dwell only on the affective and enjoyable aspects of sexual intercourse. It's not an end unto itself that should be sought independently. The Old Testament contains rules that regulate the expression of one's sexuality. Adultery and fornication are forbidden and severely punished by divine law. This prohibition, and punishment for its violation, is made clear:

> If a man is discovered lying with a woman who is married to another, they both shall die, the man who was lying with the woman as well as the woman. Thus shall you purge the evil from Israel.
>
> If there is a young woman, a virgin who is betrothed, and a man comes upon her in the city and lies with her, you shall bring them both out

> to the gate of the city and there stone them to death… (Deuteronomy 22:22–24)

In the Old Testament, adultery is a violation of the sixth commandment: *"You shall not commit adultery"* (Exodus 20:14). This calls for severe punishment of both partners (Leviticus 18:20, 20:10, Deuteronomy 5:18, Exodus 20:14).

According to Kasenene, "The severity of the punishment suggests that adultery is viewed not just as a private violation of the spouses' right to exclusive sexual enjoyment of the partner, but also as a serious threat to the fabric of society."[35]

Adultery isn't the only act that is forbidden. Fornication and premarital sex are also to be punished.

Female virginity was greatly valued in Israel and scripture provides a concrete example of the severe punishment that was to be inflicted on a maiden who was found not to be a virgin at marriage:

> If a man, after marrying a woman and having relations with her, comes to dislike her, and accuses her of misconduct and slanders her by saying, "I married this woman, but when I approached her I did not find evidence of her virginity," the father and mother of the young woman shall take the evidence of her virginity and bring it to the elders at the city gate. There the father of the young woman shall say to the elders, "I gave

---

[35] Kasenene, *Religious Ethics in Africa*, 62.

my daughter to this man in marriage, but he has come to dislike her, and now accuses her of misconduct, saying: 'I did not find evidence of your daughter's virginity.' But here is the evidence of my daughter's virginity!" And they shall spread out the cloth before the elders of the city. Then these city elders shall take the man and discipline him, and fine him one hundred silver shekels, which they shall give to the young woman's father, because the man slandered a virgin in Israel... But if this charge is true, and evidence of the young woman's virginity is not found, they shall bring the young woman to the entrance of her father's house and there the men of her town shall stone her to death, because she committed a shameful crime in Israel by prostituting herself in her father's house. (Deuteronomy 22:13–21)

As in many African cultures, as revealed in the previous chapter, the virginity of young women at marriage is held in great esteem. So it was for the people of the Old Testament. Any failure to practice this virtue would have incurred severe punishment.

But should this punishment have included the death penalty? We have no record stating that young women were stoned to death. However, it is believed that the death penalty was a cultural way of frightening youth into maintaining their virginity until marriage.

The New Testament view. The good news of the New Testament is not exclusive to what concerns human spirituality. However, it embraces all aspects of the human person, including one's sexuality. For this reason, some moralists comment,

> The principal message of the New Testament is that the long-awaited good news heralded by the prophets, is now at hand. God himself, through Jesus, is establishing his kingdom of justice, peace and love, bringing his peoples and all mankind redemption and salvation and, most wonderfully and unexpectedly, making possible a kind of intimate friendship with himself. This good news brings with it radical moral demands, and put everything in a new light including Human sexuality.[36]

According to this perspective, the general position found across the New Testament with regard to premarital sex is that it is morally wrong because it constitutes a misuse of one's body, which is the temple of the Holy Spirit (1 Corinthians 6:12–20).

In some gospel passages, Jesus referred respectively to the Old Testament to show that the sexual differentiation of male and female has always been part of the plan of creation (Matthew 19:4, Genesis 1:27; Mark 10:6, Genesis 2:24). Therefore, the only proper context for genital activity is in marriage. If people indulge in intercourse in marriage, according to the gospel's teaching, it follows that neither adultery nor premarital sex is to be allowed or encouraged among unmarried people, especially youth (John 8:3–11).

---

[36] Lawler, Boyle, and May, *Catholic Sexual Ethics*, 24.

One cannot bypass St. Paul in dealing with sexual morality in the New Testament:

> Avoid immorality. Every other sin a person commits is outside the body, but the immoral person sins against his own body. Do you not know that your body is a temple of the holy Spirit within you, whom you have from God, and that you are not your own? For you have been purchased at a price. Therefore glorify God in your body. (1 Corinthians 6:18–20)

In fact, according to St. Paul, immorality extends to all forms of sins that result from adultery, prostitution, sodomy, and fornication. For that matter, he maintains that those who commit such sins, and many others, cannot inherit the kingdom of God.

> Do not be deceived; neither fornicators nor idolaters nor adulterers nor boy prostitutes nor sodomites nor thieves nor the greedy nor drunkards nor slanderers nor robbers will inherit the kingdom of God. (1 Corinthians 6:9–10)

Among the many sexual vices to be avoided, fornication is the most frequently mentioned; it is said to be the *"works of the flesh"* (Galatians 5:19), in opposition to the works of the Holy Spirit (Galatians 5:22).

Hence, both the gospels and Pauline letters clearly condemn premarital sex, also called fornication. According to the New Testament, those who obstinately indulge in these practices fatally inflict upon themselves the most severe spiritual punishment: self-exclusion from the kingdom and love of God. Sexual beings are called to be disciples of Jesus, but they must live out their sexual existence without sin. Even though we are sexual beings, God wants us to be as holy as himself:

> This is the will of God, your holiness: that you refrain from immorality, that each of you know how to acquire a wife for himself in holiness and honor, not in lustful passion as do the Gentiles who do not know God; not to take advantage of or exploit a brother in this matter... (1 Thessalonians 4:3–6)

HUMAN SEXUALITY IN THE CHRISTIAN TRADITION

The long Catholic theological tradition, developed over centuries, emerged as a response to specific situations in which Christians of specific times found themselves. The early Christians lived amidst the Greco-Roman world in an age of great sexual licentiousness. Debauchery and disregard for human life prevailed. These Christians were challenged by Ghnosticism, a metaphysical dualistic teaching that extended the "evilness" of matter to human sexuality, consequently despising procreation through marital intercourse.[37]

---

[37] Ibid., 32.

It was precisely in this context of sexual immorality and gnostic contempt for the generation of new life through sexual intercourse that the fathers of the church wrote in order to instruct faithful Christians about the goodness of human sexuality by emphasizing its procreative function.

To account for this, Justin the Martyr said, "But whether we marry, it is only that we may bring up children; or whether we decline marriage, we live continently... promiscuous intercourse is not one of our mysteries."[38]

Interestingly, some church fathers, such as Gregory of Nyssa, John Chrysostom, and Theodoret, were suspicious of the human sexual appetite, which they thought became operative only after the fall of Adam and Eve. However, this doesn't render sexual activity evil in itself. These fathers realized that sexual desire easily leads some to fornication. That is why Lactantius and John Chrysostom, taking for granted that sexual intercourse is only morally right in marriage, were of the opinion that "marital relations may rightly be chosen in order to alleviate sexual desire and avoid fornication."[39]

The theological reflections of St. Augustine take a rather pessimistic view of sex, especially concerning concupiscence. According to him, concupiscence underlies the original sin and even serves as its principal source. However, St. Augustine also recognized the goodness of human sexuality and maintained that only marriage provides the standard for proper sexual activity. More than that, he taught that any sexual intercourse that doesn't aim at procreation is a sin.

---

[38] Justin the Martyr, *Martyr, Apology I*, 29.

[39] Lawler, Boyle, and May, *Catholic Sexual Ethics*, 35.

Many medieval theologians got straight to the point in teaching that any premarital sex is sinful and immoral. For Peter Lombard, for instance, premarital sex was a grave and sinful violation of the sixth commandment.[40]

The general position of the Catholic tradition, as well as other Christian denominations, is clear: premarital sex is a violation of both the natural moral law written in the heart of humankind and the divine moral law revealed to us in scripture. Christian tradition maintains that believers and nonbelievers alike must avoid this sinful, immoral, and irresponsible act, especially in cases where intercourse doesn't lead to procreation and the upbringing of children.

This position of the church is recalled in Thomas Aquinas's opinion on premarital sex:

> Nonmarital sexual union is contrary to the demands of the natural law insofar as it acts against the good of offspring. "The end of the exercise of the genital organs is the generation and education of children; therefore, every exercise of these powers which is not properly ordered to the generation of the children and the education to which they have a right is itself disordered." Thus, the sexual intercourse outside of marriage is excluded, for it is only in marriage that human life can properly be given, matured, and educated in the love and worship of God.[41]

---

[40] Peter Lombard, *Libri IV Sententiarum III*, 37.

[41] Lawler, Boyle, and May, *Catholic Sexual Ethics*, 45.

THE MAGISTERIAL TEACHING ON HUMAN SEXUALITY

Human sexuality is numbered among the countless gifts God has given his people for their own good and assumes a threefold function—it is relational, erotic, and procreative.[42]

Every human being has the capacity to be affectionate and therefore enter into relationships with others, be they friendly or intimate. From this perspective, it becomes clear that human sexuality is

> an important ingredient of our being relational persons. Although it can be the source of great joy and pleasure for us, the fulfillment of that joy does not lie in self-pleasuring but in the mutual enjoyment of relational intimacy as human persons.[43]

Moreover, sexuality has a loving dimension, presenting "a way of relating and being open to others; through a love that is donation and acceptance, love as giving and receiving."[44]

The tradition of the church has been that the primary end of sexual intercourse is meant to be procreation, which therefore excludes all forms of premarital sex. However, some people advocate for premarital sex arguing that it is an expression of love that

---

[42] Xavier Thevenol, *New Developments in Sexual Morality* (Rome, IT: Concilium, 1984), 83–84.

[43] Kevin T. Kelly, *New Directions in Sexual Ethics: Moral Theology and the Challenge of AIDS* (London, UK: Cassell, 1998), 146.

[44] Pontifical Council for the Family, *The Truth and Meaning of Human Sexuality* (Nairobi, KE: Paulines Publications Africa, 1998), 11.

exists between a young man and woman. If love must reside at the core of any sexual intercourse for it to be morally justifiable, it has to take place in the context of a lifelong commitment.

Vincent Genovesi shared the same view:

> It is not simply any form of true love therefore, that provided the necessary context for genital sexuality [sexual intercourse] but rather only that true love which is strong and free and courageous enough to invest itself in a pledge or commitment… sexual union should occur within the context of a life commitment because the body-giving involved in physical intercourse at the same time expresses the self-giving and spirit-sharing that are the essence of love.[45]

Beyond the procreative function of sexual intercourse, the recent magisterium of the church emphasizes another end: the unitive function of sex. This purpose is not sought independently, however. It must be coupled with the procreative function of sexuality.

Pope Paul VI underlined the inseparability of these two functions:

> That teaching, often set forth by the magisterium, is founded upon the inseparable connection

---

[45] Vincent J. Genovesi, *In Pursuit of Love: Catholic Morality and Human Sexuality* (Collegeville, MN: The Liturgical Press, 1996), 150–154.

willed by God and unable to be broken by man on his own initiative, between the two meanings of the conjugal act: the unitive meaning and the procreative meaning. Indeed, by its intimate structure, the conjugal act, while most closely uniting husband and wife, capacitates them for the generation of new lives, according to laws inscribed in the very being of man and woman. By safeguarding both these essential aspects, the unitive and the procreative, the conjugal act preserves in its fullness the sense of true mutual love and its ordination towards man's most high calling to parenthood.[46]

Here again, the inseparability of the procreative and unitive functions of sexual intercourse finds its proper exercise in the social and divine covenant of marriage. Hence, there can be no claim that premarital sex is permissible on the grounds of its erotic function alone. Any sexual intercourse that separates the procreative and unitive significance of sexuality may be human, but it is not Christian.

THE IMMORALITY OF SEXUAL ACTIVITIES

Many sexual activities—such as adultery, fornication, prostitution, rape, incest, and masturbation—can be considered to be immoral. But it is much more interesting to examine the grounds by which the church judges all forms of premarital sex immoral.

[46] Paul VI, *Humanae Vitae* (Rome, IT: Catholic Truth Society, 1968), 12.

The following comment of Catholic moralists provides us with sufficient information as far as the magisterial position is concerned:

> In proclaiming the norms of sexual behavior rooted in God's law, the Magisterium has always taught that it is seriously wrong to choose to engage in any sexual activity that is not authentically marital. From the first days of the church, pastoral leaders taught, as scripture had, that those who engage in fornication [or premarital sex] gross indecency and sexual irresponsibility… will not inherit the kingdom of God.[47]

The teaching of the magisterium regarding the morality of sexual activity aims to restrict sexual intimacy to those in the lifelong commitment of marriage. In doing so, the church seeks to preserve the value of sexual intercourse and therefore foster human dignity in intimate relationships, and rightly so.

Pope John Paul II made this position clear:

> The only place in which this self-giving in its whole truth is made possible is marriage, the covenant of conjugal love freely and consciously chosen, whereby man and woman accept the intimate community of life and love willed by God

---

[47] Lawler, Boyle, and May, *Catholic Sexual Ethics*, 64.

himself; which only in this light manifests its true meaning.[48]

The main teachings of the three sources of theology pertaining to sex have a common denominator: they indicate that sex is properly reserved for marital relationships in which the shared love of a couple takes the form of a lifelong commitment. Marriage is therefore the only context in which the full richness of human sexual love can be achieved, because "just as God's love is creative and faithful, so also should human sexual love, when genitally expressed, be open to procreation and expressive of unity and permanent fidelity."[49]

In sum, premarital sex has no sufficient grounds to be considered permissible, because it is neither a genuine reflection of the creative and eternal love of God for humankind nor is it a deliberate act that leads to procreation.

---

[48] John Paul II, *Familiaris Consortio* (Rome, IT: Catholic Truth Society, 1981), 11.

[49] Genovesi, *In Pursuit of Love*, 180.

CHAPTER FOUR

PRACTICAL SUGGESTIONS
— FOR THE CHALLENGE OF —
PREMARITAL SEX AMONG YOUTH

> Do you not know that your
> body is a temple of the holy
> Spirit within you, whom you
> have from God, and that you
> are not your own? For you
> have been purchased at a
> price. Therefore glorify God
> in your body. (1 Corinthians
> 6:19–20)

MANY PEOPLE TODAY, whether young or old, continue to wrongly believe that virginity at marriage is irrelevant. It remains an important virtue that is promoted in every culture and religion.

REASONS FOR LIVING THE VIRTUE OF VIRGINITY

Considering both the Christian and African understanding of human sexuality in general, and their views on premarital sex in particular, we come to the conclusion that any sexual activity practiced before marriage is out of place in a young person's life. It goes without saying therefore that youth are recommended to remain virginal before marriage.

Why does both Christian and African tradition maintain that virginity is still an important value for young men and women today?

According to the teaching of the Catholic church, there is no compromise with regard to premarital sex. Just as no unbaptized person or child under the age of reason can be allowed to receive holy communion, young people must not enjoy the sexual privileges that constitute the sacrament of matrimony. Sex is reserved only for couples who have committed themselves to the lifelong covenant of marriage.

Both Christian and African traditions value virginity because it prepares young people to practice fidelity in their future marriages, which will inevitably produce circumstances that call for discipline and faithfulness, such as a spouse's sickness or periods of separation. Those who aren't trained to remain chaste may fall into unfaithfulness. In order to prevent divorce, which can result from infidelity, these traditions insist on premarital virginity.

Another important reason to promote a culture of virginity among youth today is the tremendous damage that is wrought by sexually transmitted infections in many parts of the world, especially developing countries. Despite the utilization of condoms, the death rate of young people around the world due to STIs remains significant. Both scientists and religious leaders recognize that the most effective way to prevent these infections, including HIV/AIDs, is abstinence. Advocating for abstinence is another way of telling youth to remain virginal until they are ready to commit themselves to marriage.

The young and old alike consider life to be the most precious gift. It needs to be lived with great care. Therefore, the quality of a person's life reveals a lot about their personality. Young people, for instance, are to live worthy of praise and admiration. Among such people, very few spend most of their time in pubs and bars dancing, drinking, and sleeping with others. Their self-respect is a fundamental quality.

One of the surest ways young people can achieve this type of life is to practice self-discipline regarding sexual behaviour and pursue the virtue of virginity.

Everybody wants to experience freedom. No one wants to be enslaved to anybody or anything. Some human behaviours, unfortunately, such as the habitual practice of sexual activity among youth, can enslave and addict us. To avoid sexual addiction and slavery among young people, they need to be trained in the ways of virtuous living.

Having outlined some of the main reasons to promote a culture of virginity among young people today, it is imperative to also discuss some practical steps we can follow to achieve this goal.

SEXUAL EDUCATION
Sexual education is not a new solution to these moral issues. However, we can look at this from a completely new perspective.

The sexual education we are currently accustomed to in many African countries doesn't extend beyond providing basic information to young people. As far as my own memories of secondary school, regarding puberty, I recall being told that boys would experience a change of voice and girls would start to menstruate. Consequently, we were told that boys could father children and girls could conceive in the event of unprotected intercourse. It was just information, though. We were given no strategies by which to manage these troublesome sexual energies.

Without ruling out the usefulness of the informational dimension of sexual education, I would like to go further by inviting young men and women to translate that information into concrete action that helps them brave the temptation to engage in sex.

Young people must personally and voluntarily resolve to:

- Cultivate friendships that don't push them to engage in sex.
- Avoid wearing clothes that are sexually provocative.
- Avoid socializing in private with members of the opposite sex for any reason.
- Avoid reading romantic books and watching pornographic films.
- Seek the advice of people who respect their bodies and live chastely.
- Engage in noble hobbies, such as sports and reading good books.

- Educate themselves about self-control and self-discipline.
- Read and meditate on the word of God.
- Turn to a spiritual director or spiritual mentor.
- Pray for the grace to maintain their virginity until marriage.

ROLE MODELS

More than ever, our youth need role models in order to help them shape their future lives. This responsibility should fall on parents, teachers, coaches, and religious leaders who can provide good examples of moral living for young people to admire and emulate.

Parents are their children's first teachers. Therefore, it is their duty to instill in their children the cultural virtue of chastity and respect for their bodies, since the body is the dwelling place of the Holy Spirit in every human being (1 Corinthians 6:18–20).

Considering that actions speak louder than words, parents are expected to lead lives of fidelity in marriage. Seeing such a positive example day after day will convince their children to remain virginal until marriage. Parents cannot succeed in convincing their children not to steal while they themselves are stealing, very often in their children's presence. In the same way, they must practice the virtue of fidelity in marriage whilst also preaching it.

Teachers are not left out in the sexual education of young people. If youth are made aware of the importance of virginity right from childhood, the work will become easier for teachers who find themselves continuing where the parents have left off.

Young people will take the matter more seriously if they see people in their lives translating this message into action.

If both parents and teachers fail to provide an effective model for youth to emulate, their next hope should be found in the example set before them by religious leaders, such as parish priests, pastors, and chaplains.

We expect that our religious leaders will display pious and chase lifestyles that encourage people in their Christian faith. For these leaders, it is a great task to accomplish, especially those involved in youth ministry. They must both preach and practice the virtue of virginity at all times (2 Timothy 4:2).

Hence, we can see that parents, educators, and religious leaders all have a significant role to play in the sexual education of young people. They all must work together for the education to be effective. Only in this way can young people get the support and encouragement they need to say no to premarital sex.

SUPPORT GROUPS

Apart from these supports, it is equally important that youth who are willing to embrace a culture of virginity come together to support and encourage one another.

Many young people engage in sexual activity as a result of peer pressure. Sometimes a good number of them feel uncomfortable among their friends for the simple reason that they have no experience of sexual intercourse.

To make young people feel comfortable with their virginal status and feel a sense of belonging, they can either start or join a support group. Such a group can be of great help to those who are virgins as well as those who for one reason or another have lost their virginity but are now resolved to keep themselves chaste until marriage. A group like this, whether in a parish setting or at a learning institution, can promote the virtue of virginity through encouraging self-discipline.

These groups are like schools where youth are trained, perhaps by youth ministers, in the virtue of chastity through daily personal effort. They need to also commit themselves to a life of prayer and remain confident in God's grace for their success.

It takes a learning process for a person to embrace the virtue of virginity. This is so beautifully said in the Catechism of the Catholic Church:

> Chastity [virginity] includes an apprenticeship in self-mastery, which is a training in human freedom. The alternative is clear: either man governs his passions and finds peace, or he lets himself be dominated by them and becomes unhappy. Man's dignity therefore requires him to act out of conscious and free choice, a moved and drawn in personal way from within and not by blind impulses in himself or by mere external constraint. Man gains such dignity when, ridding himself of all slavery to the passions, he presses forward to his goal by freely choosing what is good and, by his diligence and skill,

effectively secures for himself the means suited
to this end.[50]

The virtue of virginity demands lifelong training in self-discipline. As such,

one can never consider it acquired once and for
all. It presupposes renewed effort at all stages
of life. The effort required can be more intense
in certain periods, such as when the personality
is being formed during childhood and adoles-
cence.[51]

Apart from constant personal effort, young people must not
lose sight of the ever-present divine grace that abides with them
throughout their lives. Without this grace, they may not be able to
keep themselves virginal until marriage.

More than being a moral virtue, youth should be made to
consider virginity a divine gift that can be freely granted to them
through spiritual exercises and Christian prayer.

Members of a support group of the type I suggest can meet on
a weekly basis to share the word of God and pray collectively for the
grace of virginity until marriage. These groups are forums wherein
young people can cultivate and develop mature friendships amongst
themselves. Additionally, they can enter into a loving dynamic

---

[50] *Catechism of the Catholic Church* (Nairobi, KE: Ignatius Press, 1995), #2339.
[51] Ibid., #2342.

through developing an intimate and personal friendship with Jesus Christ.

After a period of reasonable time—for example, three months of membership—any youth who is interested can freely apply to their chaplain to request to take a yearly oath of virginity in the presence of all the other members of their group, as well as parents and a youth minister. This oath could take different formats, but it should always leave room for mentioning the youth's name, their free decision to take the oath, and their request for God to help them remain faithful to it. The following is my suggestion:

> Lord God, nothing is impossible for you. Whoever has faith in you is never deceived. With faith and confidence, I (name) swear by my free will to keep myself virginal and chaste for a period of one year as a preparation until I receive the sacrament of matrimony in the church. May God be witness to this commitment, and through the help of his grace may I live according to it.

After this commitment to virginity, youth should be expected to share among themselves the challenges they encounter in carrying it out. They can encourage one another to be faithful to their commitment. After all, to remain virginal until marriage, in this modern world that is highly influenced by advertisements of free sex, can only be the result of the combined effects of God's grace and the human discipline of self-control.

CONCLUSION

THE OBSERVATION IS clear: many young people are sexually active, but almost nobody seems to be concerned. Whether Christian or otherwise, youth today seem to have never heard the words of Solomon: *"There is an appointed time for everything, and a time for every affair under the heavens"* (Ecclesiastes 3:1). They take for granted that it is good, even advisable, to experience sex before marriage. Petting, kissing, and intimate hugging have become normal behaviours.

In fact, these behaviours seem to raise no questions. But I have felt the need to bring this issue forward. It isn't so easy to brave these cultural taboos surrounding anything having to do with sexuality in our African culture.

However, I have found out that talking about these subjects is the only way to save the current generation of young Christians who are losing their sense of moral dignity and integrity with regard to sexuality.

While exploring our African and Christian heritages in terms of human sexuality, I have discovered very inspiring teachings that promote healthy, constructive, and mature relationships between people of the opposite sex.

On the other hand, I have also discovered some traditional practices I would like to suggest should be discontinued. The idea of sexual activity serving as a form of hospitality, as well as the practice of group marriage, is to be discouraged. Not only are they incompatible with the Christian doctrine of monogamy, but they also expose people to the merciless dangers of contracting STIs, including HIV/AIDs.

The Bible's death penalty for sins of adultery and fornication ought to be revised for the simple reason that God does not wish the death of sinners but rather their conversion.

On the grounds of the positive teachings I have encountered, I feel the urgent need to draw the attention of young people to the goodness and necessity of cultivating the virtue of virginity and respect for the human body.

To the problem of premarital sex among youth, I have suggested sexual education in the concrete forms of personal self-discipline, the counsel and example of role models, intimate and personal friendship with Jesus Christ, and the spiritual help of prayer and divine grace to achieve the ultimate model of chastity.

It is my fervent hope that this booklet will be helpful for young men and women who strongly want to make a difference as Christians among their peers in keeping themselves virginal and chaste until marriage.

BIBLIOGRAPHY

Bénézet Bujo, *African Christian Morality at the Age of Inculturation*
(Nairobi, KE: Paulines Publications Africa, 1990).

Bénézet Bujo, *Foundations of an African Ethic: Beyond the Universal Claim of Western Morality* (Nairobi, KE: Paulines Publications Africa, 2003).

Catechism of the Catholic Church (Nairobi, KE: Ignatius Press,
1995).

Gerald Coleman, *Human Sexuality: An All-Embracing Gift* (New
York, NY: Alba House, 1992).

Dave Daddy, "What Is Human Sexuality and What Is Normal?" *Catholic Education*. Date of access: October 15, 2004 (http://catholiceducation.org/articles/sexuality/se0002.html).

Robert B. Fisher, *West African Religious Traditions: Focus on the Akan of Ghana* (Maryknoll, NY: Orbis Books, 1998).

Vincent J. Genovesi, *In Pursuit of Love: Catholic Morality and Human Sexuality* (Collegeville, MN: The Liturgical Press, 1996).

John Paul II, *Familiaris Consortio* (Rome, IT: Catholic Truth Society, 1981).

Justin the Martyr, *Martyr, Apology I*.

Paul VI, *Humanae Vitae* (Rome, IT: Catholic Truth Society, 1968).

Peter Kasenene, *Religious Ethics in Africa* (Kampala, UG: Fountain Publishers, 1998).

Kevin T. Kelly, *New Directions in Sexual Ethics: Moral Theology and the Challenge of AIDS* (London, UK: Cassell, 1998).

Benezeri Kisembo, Laurenti Magesa, and Aylward Shorter, *African Christian Marriage* (Nairobi, KE: Paulines Publications Africa, 1998).

Jane M. Kiura, Regina Gitau, and Andrew Kiura, *On Life and Love: Guidelines for Parents and Educators* (Nairobi, KE: Paulines Publications Africa, 1999).

Leo Kock, "Advice on Sex," *The Daily Illini*. March 18, 1960.

Ronald Lawler, Joseph Boyle, and William E. May, *Catholic Sexual Ethics: A Summary, Explanation, and Defense* (Huntington, IN: Our Sunday Visitor, 1998).

J. Lebubu, "The Youth on the Threshold of the Year 2000," *African Ecclesial Review*. February 1989.

Peter Lombard, *Libri IV Sententiarum III*.

Marjorie Oludhe Macgoye, *Moral Issues in Kenya: A Personal View* (Nairobi, KE: Uzima Publishing House, 1996).

James A. Mohler, *Love, Marriage, and the Family: Yesterday and Today* (New York, NY: Alba House, 1992).

Henry Okullu, *Church and Marriage in East Africa* (Nairobi, KE: Uzima Press, 1990).

I.D. Osabutey-Aguedze, *The African Religion and Philosophy* (Nairobi, KE: Maillu Publishing House, 1990).

A. Oyekanmi, "Understanding Sexuality in Yoruba Culture," *Africa Regional Sexuality Resource Centre*. Date of access: September 29, 2004 (http://www.arsrc.org/en/resources/reports/alaba comments.pdf).

Pontifical Council for the Family, *The Truth and Meaning of Human Sexuality* (Nairobi, KE: Paulines Publications Africa, 1998).

Sacred Congregation for Catholic Education, *Educational Guidance in Human Love* (Rome, IT: Catholic Truth Society, 1983).

Aylward Shorter, *Celibacy and African Culture* (Nairobi, KE: Paulines Publications Africa, 1998).

Janet Smith, "Premarital Sex," *Catholic Education*. Date of access: October 20, 2004 (http://catholiceducation.org/articles/sexuality/se0002.html).

Xavier Thevenol, *New Developments in Sexual Morality* (Rome, IT: Concilium, 1984).